NEED
FEEL
WRITE

Also by Pamela Sackett

Two Minutes To Shine:
Thirty Potent New Monologues for the Auditioning Actor
Two Minutes To Shine: Book II
Two Minutes To Shine: Book III
Two Minutes To Shine, Book IV:
Contemporary Monologues for Mixed Ages
Two Minutes To Shine: Book V
(Samuel French, Inc. New York)

Speak of the Ghost:
In the Name of Emotion Literacy
Saving the World Solo
Booing Death: with Shpilkes & Rhyme
I Can: Twelve Ways to Witness the Heart
(Emotion Literacy Advocates, Seattle)

NEED
FEEL
WRITE

Storied Picture Prompts
for the Brave Journaler

PAMELA SACKETT & JOHN KLOSSNER

Copyright © 2023 Pamela Sackett, John Klossner
All rights reserved.

Cartoons & captions by John Klossner; all other writing by Pamela Sackett, unless other persons are named. No part of this book may be used, reproduced or transmitted in any form or by any means whatsoever without written permission from the author, except in the case of brief quotations embodied in academic research and journals, critical articles and reviews.

Book production & cover design: Daniel Sackett
Cover art background: Megan Basaldua
Special thanks:
Canva, Catchafire, Markzware
Diana Heald, Jennifer Johnson

For information:
Emotion Literacy Advocates
www.emolit.org   info@emolit.org
emolit.org/need-feel-write-book
ISBN 978-0-929904-09-2

Toward sustainable publishing, this book is manufactured on demand to reduce supply chain waste, greenhouse emissions and conserve valuable natural resources.

This book is dedicated to
Tiffany Hannibal
"The Journaling Stan" Podcast Host

INTRODUCTION

NEED FEEL WRITE is here to serve you as food for thought and unequivocal encouragement for your own self-reflective writings.

What you will find on these pages grew out of a lucky surprise collaboration. In 2021, John Klossner entered Emotion Literacy Advocates' (ELA) world, proposed and delivered a set of cartoons prompted by Pamela Sackett's writings generated on behalf of ELA. She then responded to John's cartoons as prompts—in her nuanced, revelatory mode—with narrative portraits and related questions. Pamela's intent: to create a book that encourages journaling as a way to unfold, know and understand the essential nature and inner-workings of soft needs and the feelings that accompany them.

ELA offers this collection to the seasoned journaler, as well as those who want to begin a self-reflective practice in writing. Journaling is the epitome of such a practice—a potent avenue towards building and expanding trust in and capacity for critical-creative thinking...

...ELA dearly appreciates and unabashedly aims to bolster and endorse the journaler...here, there and everywhere. May these prompts inspire, nourish and buoy your creative expression and personal discoveries.

P.S. We highly recommend the **I Can** book, our first and foremost primer for emotion literacy fundamentals. **I Can** sets the contextual frame for **NEED FEEL WRITE** and will assist in tapping our prompts' full potential.

Dear Journaler,

I commend you for your practice of paying close attention to the details of your life. Our society benefits every time even just one individual elects to live more knowingly inside their own experience of being alive. Each one of us is uniquely human and to fully know and understand your personhood is a noble endeavor, one that merits celebration and strengthens community.

Recognizing and understanding what we need and how we feel at the core, is an incalculable, if not often supported, life skill. Insightful self-communication is key in shaping inclusive perspectives and guiding informed decisions.

Journaling offers the opportunity to slow your pace, sort and soothe what ails you and envision afresh.

I see the brave journaler as one who can take initiative, one who can dare to be curious. I see the brave journaler as one who can possess gumption, one who can think independently. I see the brave journaler as one who can witness, one who can create social change. I see the brave journaler as one who can have a hand in the vital individual and societal benefits of learning to know, communicate with and love thyself!

In fellowship, gratefully,
Pamela

Table of Contents

NOT THE HOW 19
MY COSTUME 23
SHARING HELPS 27
THE KEY'S KEEPER 31
OR IS IT THE LAW 35
ENLIGHTENED WITNESS 39
HUFFnPUFF 43
TRUE CONFESSION 47
TERMS & CONDITIONS 51
SOVEREIGN 55
YES AND... 59
UNMATCHED SET 63
DULY NOTED 67
DREAM LESSONS 71
TICKET FOR TWO 75
SOME THING 79
FLEETING HOPE 83
STOP, SENSE, LISTEN, RE-LEARN 87
CHALLENGE OF THE CENTURY 91
PIVOTAL 95
SOMEONE, PLEASE 99
TAKE TWO 103
PERFECT PARADOXICAL PAIR 107
I KNOW BETTER 111
MY VERY OWN 115

"Fill your paper with the breathings of your heart."
~William Wordsworth

Do that cute thing where you acknowledge your feelings.

NOT THE HOW

What does it mean to be a private person, what does it mean to say I know you, what does it mean to say you like me, if I never even show through my stuff? Do you want to see me, would you spend the time? Do you want to see the what that I carry, the what I carry deep inside? What does it mean to come out? Will you want to block, fix or witness and if I don't pass your litmus, will my other colors have to hide?

What does "cute" mean to you,
when used in this way?

Can you think of another way, or two or three, of saying "I don't care what people think" that makes what's between the lines of that declaration more clear?

Suggestion: employ "because..."

Brandon does this neat trick where he acts completely different than he's feeling.

MY COSTUME

I tap danced my way through childhood. Theatrical performance came easy and so did compliance. Intuition was my choreographer. I sensed what the situation called for and delivered. It took me years to discover how tight the tailoring, how tangled the threads. The trickiest part was finding out how I truly felt about the whole enterprise.

Make note of the time your behavior
and your feeling did not match.

Examples: anger on the outside,
disappointment & hurt on the inside
jovial on the outside,
uneasy & anxious on the inside

Was the mis-match intentional or were you unaware of it at the time?

I'd love to hear your feelings, but I'm afraid
that would cause me to have feelings.

SHARING HELPS

The most difficult thing, for me, about feelings is not when they gush in plain view. Not when they genuinely unravel. I've never known one of my essential feelings to sit quietly when hidden nor have they ever agreed to evaporate. Though my decisive, black and white notions, that I automatically conjure and promptly apply, do a great job cutting off their oxygen supply, my feelings indubitably emerge. Unadulterated feelings are never the problem.

Describe two scenarios; one that prompted your experience of empathy and one that prompted your experience of sympathy.

Describe a time when a person of influence in your life validated your feelings.

I forgot I had this feeling!

THE KEY'S KEEPER

What's more, I didn't know I could have a feeling like this...or would.

I had only thoughts telling me the feeling should go away. My thoughts were under-cover too. What else could my tender feeling do? Barbed-wire, clandestine beliefs kept it hiding, intricate defenses obscuring, dividing.

Until my body told the tale. The body knows, without fail, the story.

Describe a time when your thoughts led you to an insight about one of your non-physical (soft) needs.*

*Examples: to belong, to be heard, to connect.

Describe a time when
your thoughts led you
to explore & understand
an uncomfortable
feeling.

Can you identify the feeling you were harboring?

OR IS IT THE LAW?

When I ask my husband why he
refuses to tell me how he feels,
he protests my insistence that
he is withholding. "If I knew how
I felt, I would tell you." I am always
amazed to keep rediscovering just
how slippery feelings can be and
how widespread our ability to elude,
confuse and mistake them.

Describe a time you learned something significant about yourself after your behavior was misunderstood by someone close to you.

Describe a time you learned something significant about yourself after your behavior was misunderstood by you.

Just so you know, my childhood memories will be joining us tonight.

ENLIGHTENED WITNESS

I shared some of my most significant history with an artist friend and colleague. She expressed a unique kind of empathy that shifted my perception, giving those most heartrending of incidents greater gravity in my way of seeing myself. It opened a monumental door towards self-knowledge and understanding...a crystal clear view of facets of myself with which I had been keeping company, unbeknownst to me, for years.

Explore the first time you remember someone in your world validating the way you felt when you were upset.

Dig up a picture of yourself from an earlier time, ask your younger self a question and respond.

Maybe you should try a different way to express what you're feeling.

HUFFnPUFF

Maybe you should try a different way to think about my expression... maybe you should go a few rounds at my Fahrenheit...maybe you should find another way to interact with me that doesn't flaunt your impulse to control...maybe you should accept me as I am...maybe you should be a better role model...

Make an observation about a time you advocated for one of your soft needs* and another time when you did not.

*Examples: to be valued, to value, to love & to be loved.

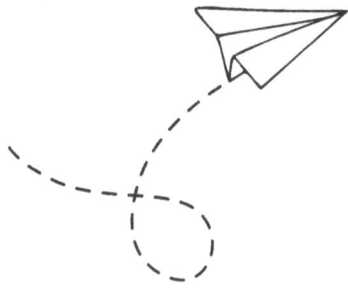

Why, in both instances?

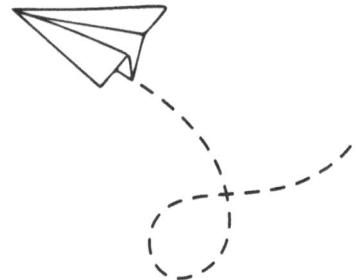

If I tell you I'm feeling a little irritable it takes all the thrill out of sniping at you.

TRUE CONFESSION

My knee jerks when I am reminded
how soft I am between-the-lines,
how porous, how malleable, how
edgy...countless unpredictabilities,
in the throes of pressing needs.
Barking seems to give me a charge
when I'm caught in that depleting
squeeze, boiling over.

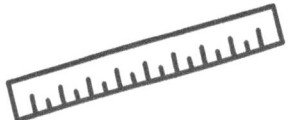

Identify one situation that is pushing you to your limit...describe what you need that is going unmet.

How are you expressing your need, to yourself and another person?

That's not a sin. That's an emotion.

TERMS & CONDITIONS

It took me an eternity to find my dictionary and when I discovered it, I saw that it had been written for me. I discovered it was filled with ideas that were not my own and that those ideas marked my beginnings and accompanied me, quite closely, for years. Lo and behold, I discovered I could re-write my dictionary so that I would recognize my feelings, what they mean to me, nearer to their start. And, so I would always know their essence and so I would always know, after a heated moment misbegets my behavior, their true & honorable definition.

Unearth a conflictual interaction when one of your comments was inaccurately recounted and reacted to by someone close to you.

Did you retrieve your own understanding of the interaction and communicate it...if not with the other person, with yourself?

I'm afraid that if I share my vulnerabilities they become part of the pubic domain.

SOVEREIGN

There are no secrets and yet I try to hide my tender self from misunderstanding eyes, especially ones that multiply. Save for those times I gather myself and dare show those parts, lay them bare, for all to see. The risk is great but self-smothering riskier. I have to speak up, I have to, it's very clear. I must be out, out from within. My walls could topple, my skin wear thin...voice: my most trusted protection.

Describe a benefit you experience from being a vulnerable human being.

Identify a goal that is worth risking your efforts to attempt.

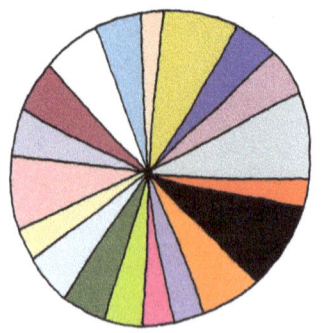

the spectrum
of feelings

the newsworthy
spectrum
of feelings

YES AND...

I remain amazed how quickly
I default to caution, to the darkest
corners of my imagination, to fear.
How sustained my alliance to the
hard-wired call of safety. So active
my story stylus, zipping fluently
between the landscape poles.
Diagramming danger on well-worn
trumpeting tracks, I turn.

What facet of one of your relationships and its circumstance incites fear and why?

What does your self-talk consist of when you are afraid and what are ways you would like to change or expand upon it?

Haven't you heard? Emotions are a thing!

UNMATCHED SET

I have no exact recollection the moment I split, the moment I stopped sitting squarely inside of it, inside of me.

The process was gradual with some sharp corners. I learned and eventually became quite adept at emoting as prescribed by a certain circle of primary sway. To behave one way and feel another—my ticket to room and board.

Recount a time when you subdued what you know about yourself to be true and subdued how you truly felt in that given moment.

In what ways did that influence your behavior?

Not on the first date.

DULY NOTED

When I first met my husband, I had no idea
I would be marrying his whole family, how
often they would show up in our moments.
There's his father in his big-hearted hands,
his sister in his inflections, pronounced
shoulders and vocal tones, his brothers in his
postural stances, sense of irony, laughter, his
mother in his music and modest ways.
Lines blur.

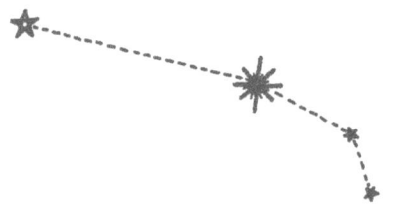

For what family traits that you carry into your current life are you grateful?

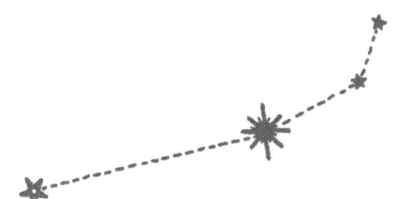

What family traits do you aspire to change and why?

I had a bad dream that you weren't worrying about me.

DREAM LESSONS

I worried about my mother for years
and even in her forever slumber,
I want to know: does she know how
much I love her? Her ready radar
and nuanced sense of humor
forever teaching.

If one of your relatives could come back to life,
what would you want to communicate
to that person?

What would you like to hear that person
say to you for the first time?

I used to be miserable. I was happy then.

TICKET FOR TWO

Grief and gratitude share a place at my table. That wasn't always the case. It took me a while to admit they deservedly take turns occupying space. When I am plagued by a situation that I didn't exactly choose and then receive an unexpected call with exhilarating news, I must again proclaim: "mutual inclusivity" rules!

Describe a loss—what it means to you and your life—that also contains within it a gain.

Can you imagine offering space for your feelings despite an unwanted situation that prompted them?

Your new normal is my old repugnant.

SOME THING

I always wanted to be a cheerleader. Buoyancy and an exuberant spirit came easy. And, I had extensive dance training from age five so I do not think I lacked grace. Apparently, I was missing some thing. Blond hair, closer-to-the-ground height, definable style, unwavering self-assurance?

Reflect upon three main influences in regards to your self confidence, both privately and in social settings.

What are the differences in your
confidence levels between the private
and the social contexts?

I find your emotional range to be pretty limited.

FLEETING HOPE

When I think of my dearly departed closest relatives, it's a heart-yank every time. Some part of me still cannot believe that I will never hear their voices or see them again. When, on not so few or far between occasions, I have an impulse to pick up the phone and call one of them, it actually takes me more than a moment to suspend disbelief.

Describe a confusing and complex exchange you had with one of your now departed relatives and see whether you can glean a new insight from that exchange.

What would you like to share with that relative about your current life?

They're good for walks and treats. But they don't know squat about reading body language.

STOP, SENSE, LISTEN, RE-LEARN

My body tends to be pretty soft-spoken but it never hesitates to send a signal when I've been remiss in meeting its needs, namely, consistently-timed deposits of whole food and rest, along with a frequent, voluntary flow of un-shallow feeling-full breathing. When I don't heed the signal, the signal promptly becomes a flare and, before I know it, those sneaky infusions of fear-driven cortisol unleash a neurological blare and shut me down for the count.

Explore recurring circumstances that incite breath-holding.

Write a letter to your fear.

Well, I don't suffer people who don't suffer fools gladly!

CHALLENGE OF THE CENTURY

How wide a reach is needed, how deep, how long? What kind of notes and how to arrange them to sing the unconditional love song. I feel my voice tightening, crackling, receding when you could not see, nor did you seem to care about the fact that I was bleeding. In plain view. Open my heart to you?

Describe a time when you began to explain to someone something of great importance to you and that someone negated its relevance.

What are a couple ways you support and reassure yourself in the absence of social support?

It's impressive what some people will do to avoid talking about their feelings.

PIVOTAL

I don't recall anyone asking me how I felt, when I was a child...or a teen. I don't remember asking myself. I do vividly remember, when I was quite young, running into my bedroom crying after something my mother said to me and my father following close behind. He knelt down at my bedside and with the tip of his finger dabbed a tear from the stream
and, oh so dearly, tasted it.

Recount a time when the value of your internal experience was reflected back to you by someone, without question.

Recount a time when you reflected back someone's internal experience & acknowledged it to that person as valuable.

His last words were 'Make up something that makes me sound profound.'

SOMEONE, PLEASE

I would say I'm never at a loss for words.
I would say my all-time greatest loss is
when my words are misinterpreted.
I would say a greater loss, still, is when my
words fall on inattentive ears.
I would say my final wish is for world-wide
everlasting communication clarity!

Reflect upon a topic close to your heart that you would dearly like to discuss with someone, not knowing whether they will understand your perspective.

Write out a dialogue that you fear you would have with that someone and a second dialogue you wish to have with that same person.

It's not pronouns I have problems with, it's the adjectives that get me in trouble.

TAKE TWO

I would like to dispense with certain descriptive words because I know they are short-sighted, incomplete and skewed. Despite this knowledge, I spew these descriptions—in the privacy of my own home or car—and my tension deflates. My body can only contain so much. Promptly thereafter, my relationship to the triggering situation rears its transparent head and clarity, if not situational cure, is mine for the claiming.

Make up a list of encouraging ways you support, or would like to support, your quest for self-knowledge.

What are some ways you discourage your inclination to be curious and ways you encourage it?

I see marriage as a verb,
he sees it as a triathlon.

PERFECT PARADOXICAL PAIR

I am grateful my husband's basic nature is gloriously different from my own, as long as our stress levels don't bypass our limits' edges. When they do, our coping strategies announce their arrival, our disparate family of origin survival dynamics leading their way. Steadfast marital foundation firmly in place, thanks to our differences, has the final say.

How do you define selfhood and who in your world reinforces the value of developing your selfhood and in what ways?

How does your uniqueness, or how do your differences, contribute to one of your close friend's lives and vice versa?

My emotional intelligence can beat up your emotional intelligence.

I KNOW BETTER

I'm deeply concerned about the acute state of polarization in our society. The on/off, stop/go, positive/negative, win/lose, right/wrong, good/bad quick fixes of our fast-paced-absolutist-survival brains and their limited and limiting narrative capacities. I would like nothing more than to turn off this wrong and bad way of going about our lives. I want that part of our brains to stop dictating the way things go, right now! I insist we immediately, at all times, adopt open-ended, brand new ways of thinking, period!

Describe the most inclusive ways you can regard your version of the human condition.

In what ways do you face or not face
the face of inevitable uncertainty?

It's always a battle of wits with them, and I arrive unarmed.

MY VERY OWN

When I was a little girl, my mother repeatedly instructed: "keep your wits about you!" I never quite knew what she meant but I made every attempt to abide. My mother embraced the spirit of competition and I rebelled. If that's what she meant by keeping my wits about me, I failed. Some years ago, one of my mother's cousins told me that, when I was a little girl, I would sit in a corner of the room quietly observing everyone there. She said she had the distinct feeling that I knew exactly what was going on. Maybe I hadn't failed my mother's instruction after all.

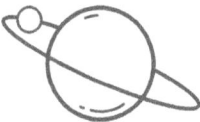

What ways of identifying yourself have accompanied you since childhood?

In what ways do these self-impressions and group identity memberships continue to feed & challenge you?

CONNECT w/EMOLIT.ORG

for more innovative arts-based
RESOURCES

free downloads

books

multi-media learning tools

including vignettes

& songbook movies

workshops + consultations

plus podcast episodes

featuring Pamela w/hosts

in lively conversations

VISIT ELA's
YouTube channel & Instagram
@emotionliteracyadvocates

Image by Srishti Dokras
from
"Passageway Songbook Movie"
(virtual musical picture book)

www.ingramcontent.com/pod-product-compliance
Lightning Source LLC
Chambersburg PA
CBHW040553010526
44110CB00054B/2664